F.P. Q

AR 2.9
0.5

Holiday Histories

Columbus Day

Mir Tamim Ansary

Heinemann Library
Chicago, Illinois

Customer Service 888-454-2279
Visit our website at www.heinemannraintree.com

Designed by Kimberly Miracle and Q2A Creative
Printed in China by South China Printing Company

10 09 08 07 06
10 9 8 7 6 5 4 3 2 1

New edition ISBNs: 1-4034-8883-5 (hardcover)
                            1-4034-8896-7 (paperback)

The Library of Congress has cataloged the first edition as follows:
Ansary, Mir Tamim.
    Columbus Day / Mir Tamim Ansary.
       p. cm. -- (Holiday histories)
    Includes bibliographical references and index.
    Summary: Introduces Columbus Day, explaining the historical events behind it, how it became a holiday, and how it is observed.
    ISBN 1-57572-702-1 (lib. bdg.)
    1. Columbus Day – Juvenile literature. 2. Columbus, Christopher – Juvenile literature. 3. America – Discovery and exploration – Spanish – Juvenile literature. [1. Columbus Day. 2. Columbus, Christopher. 3. Explorers. 4. America – Discovery and exploration – Spanish. 5. Holidays] I. Title. II. Series: Ansary, Mir Tamim. Holiday histories.

E120 .A67 1998
394.264 – dc21
                                        9813721

Acknowledgments
The author and publishers are grateful to the following for permission to reproduce photographs: Getty Images p. 5 (AFP); The Granger Collection pp. 6, 10, 12, 15, 16, 17, 19, 21, 22, 23; Natural History Museum/London p. 9; Stock Boston pp. 7 (Bob Daemmrich), 26 (Bob Daemmrich); Tony Stone p. 11 (Richard A. Cooke III); SuperStock pp. 14, 18, 24; Photo Edit pp. 20 (Anna E. Zuckerman), 25 (David Young Wolff), 27 (John Neubauer); Science Photo Library p. 29.

Cover photograph reproduced with permission of Photodisc/Getty Images.
Map Illustrator: Yoshi Miyake

Every effort has been made to contact copyright holders of any material reproduced in this book. Any omissions will be rectified in subsequent printings if notice is given to the publisher.

Disclaimer
All the Internet addresses (URLs) given in this book were valid at the time of going to press. However, due to the dynamic nature of the Internet, some addresses may have changed, or sites may have changed or ceased to exist since publication. While the author and publisher regret any inconvenience this may cause readers, no responsibility for any such changes can be accepted by either the author or the publisher.

Contents

Some words are shown in bold, **like this**. You can
find out what they mean by looking in the glossary.

A Noisy Parade

There is a noisy parade downtown today. It happens every year on the second Monday in October. Many people in this parade are Italian American, for this is Columbus Day.

Many cities have a Columbus Day Parade. They **honor** an explorer named Christopher Columbus. He was born in Genoa, Italy, in 1451. He died in 1506.

Why Columbus Is Famous

Columbus is famous for one reason. He sailed to America in 1492. Many people say that Columbus **discovered** America.

These **Native Americans** are **protesting** the idea that Columbus discovered America.

This is not true. Columbus did not get here first. America was already full of people when he came.

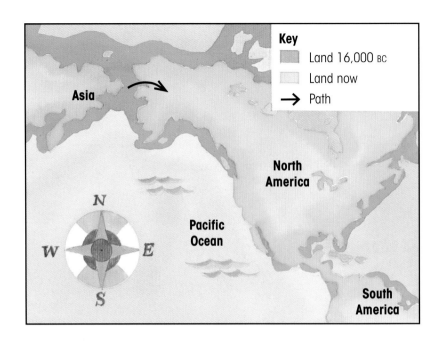

The First Americans

The first Americans came from Asia long, long ago. These people walked to America. A strip of land connected the two **continents** back then.

Over time, water covered the strip of land. The Americas were then cut off from the rest of the world.

Two Separate Worlds

Thousands of years passed. People in Europe, Asia, and Africa built great cities. The people in those cities did not know about the Americas.

Great cities were also built in the Americas. The people in these cities knew about each other. But they knew nothing of the other **continents**.

Europeans Explore

About five hundred years ago, some **Europeans** became great sailors. They wanted to sail to the islands east of India. Those lands were called the **Indies**.

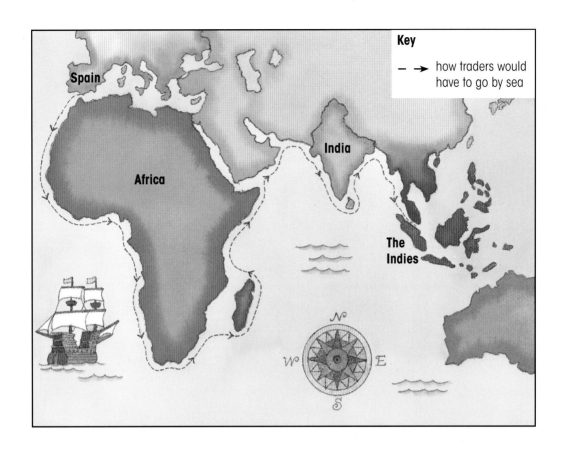

Traders had reached the Indies by land. They had brought back spices, silk, and other rich **goods**. But no one had reached the Indies by sea. The trip was too long.

A Crazy Idea

Christopher Columbus knew the world was round. He had an idea. Why not get to the **Indies** by sailing west? It might be quicker, thought Columbus.

Most people called Columbus crazy. They said
the ocean was too big to cross. They said sea
monsters would get him.

A Queen Listens

But one person listened. She was Isabella, queen of Spain. She wanted the **goods** of the **Indies**. She hoped Columbus would find a shortcut to those islands. She decided to help him.

Isabella gave Columbus three ships. They were called the *Nina*, the *Pinta*, and the *Santa Maria*. She gave him 90 sailors. Columbus headed out to sea.

Crossing the Ocean

He sailed for weeks. His sailors got scared. They begged Columbus to turn back. Columbus said no. The sailors were about to kill him when . . .

. . . they spotted an island! Columbus thought it was part of the **Indies**. He called the people who lived there "Indians."

A New World

Columbus had landed in the Bahamas, hundreds of miles from what is now Florida. West of these islands lay North and South America. **Europeans** had never seen these **continents**.

After Columbus, many Europeans sailed to the "New World." **Priests** came to spread the Christian religion. Soldiers came to find gold.

Europeans Take Over

Europeans spread all over the Americas. They cut down forests and planted **crops**. They built new cities. They tried out new ways of life.

The Europeans fought with the **Native Americans**. They destroyed many Native American cities. European **germs** killed many Native Americans.

The Native Americans

But **Europeans** also learned from the **Native Americans**. They learned about new foods, such as potatoes, corn, squash, peppers, and turkey.

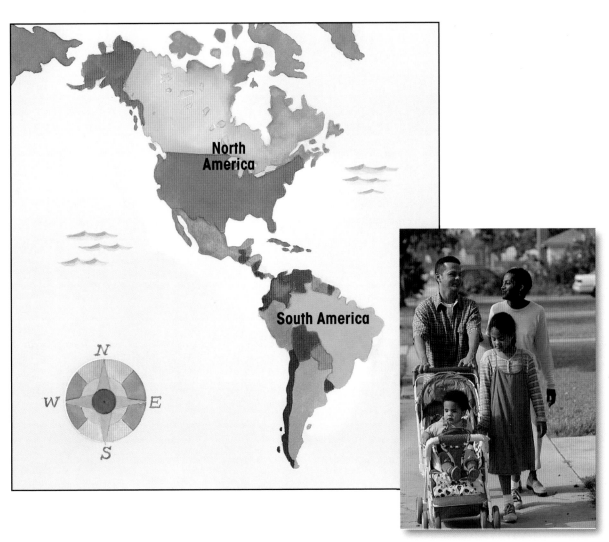

Some Europeans mixed with the Native Americans. Out of the mixture came new people. Thirty-five new nations rose in the Americas. One of them is our country.

Celebrating Columbus Day

Columbus Day was first celebrated in Colorado in 1907. Today it is a national holiday.

These are **replicas** of Columbus' ships in Corpus Christi, Texas.

Columbus Day is also celebrated in many other countries. In Costa Rica it is called Culture Day.

Into the Unknown

Today the whole world has been mapped. But there is still much to explore. Look up at the night sky. You are looking into the **unknown**.

Columbus sailed into the unknown without fear.
We still need his spirit. We are still exploring.
That is why we celebrate Columbus Day.

This picture was taken on Mars by the
Mars Exploration Rover *Spirit* in 2004.

Important Dates

Columbus Day

30,000 BC–10,000 BC	First Americans come from Asia
around 1400	**Europeans** begin to explore the world
1451	Christopher Columbus is born
1492	Columbus sails to America
1506	Columbus dies
1907	Colorado celebrates the first Columbus Day

Glossary

continents   large land areas of the Earth

crops   plants grown by farmers for food and other uses

discovered   find something that no one knew about

Europeans   people from Europe

germs   tiny life forms that make people sick

goods   things people use

honor   show respect for something or someone

Indies   Indonesia and other islands east of India

Native Americans   another name for American Indians

priests   leaders in a Christian church

protesting   showing that you disagree with something

replicas   copies of something

unknown   something that we know nothing about

Find Out More

Ansary, Mir Tamim. *Southeast Indians.* Chicago: Heinemann Library, 2000.

Krensky, Stephen. *Christopher Columbus.* New York: Random House, 2003.

Lynch, Emma. *We're From Italy.* Chicago: Heinemann Library, 2005.

Index